ON LINE

J.975.80.
Davis
Davis, Mary, 1934-

The Georgia colony /

THE *Georgia* COLONY

Our Thirteen Colonies

SPIRIT
of America®

THE *Georgia* COLONY

By Marc Davis

Content Adviser: Eric Gilg, Department of History,
University of Massachusetts, Amherst, Massachusetts

The Child's World®
Chanhassen, Minnesota

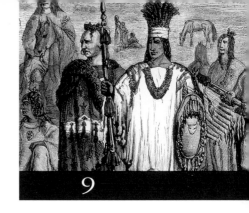
9

THE *Georgia* COLONY

Published in the United States of America by The Child's World®
PO Box 326 • Chanhassen, MN 55317-0326 • 800-599-READ • www.childsworld.com

Acknowledgments
The Child's World®: Mary Berendes, Publishing Director

Editorial Directions, Inc.: E. Russell Primm, Editorial Director; Melissa McDaniel, Line Editor; Elizabeth K. Martin, Assistant Editor; Olivia Nellums, Editorial Assistant; Susan Hindman, Copy Editor; Joanne Mattern, Proofreader; Kevin Cunningham, Peter Garnham, Ruthanne Swiatkowski, Fact Checkers; Tim Griffin/IndexServ, Indexer; Cian Loughlin O'Day, Photo Researcher; Linda S. Koutris, Photo Selector

Photo
Cover: Getty Images/Hulton Archive; Bettmann/Corbis: 20, 27, 32; Corbis: 6 (Raymond Gehman), 8 (The Burstein Collection), 10, 13 (James Randklev), 22 (Lee Snider; Lee Snider), 24, 25 (The Stapleton Collection), 35 (Joe McDonald); Getty Images/Hulton Archive: 15, 18, 21, 23, 28, 29, 30; Kevin Fleming/Corbis: 26, 34; Library of Congress, Washington D.C./Bridgeman Art Library: 12; North Wind Picture Archives: 9, 16; Stock Montage: 11, 14, 19.

Registration
The Child's World®, Spirit of America®, and their associated logos are the sole property and registered trademarks of The Child's World®.

Library of Congress Cataloging-in-Publication Data
Davis, Marc, 1934–
  The Georgia colony / by Marc Davis.
    p. cm. — (Our colonies)
"Spirit of America."
Includes bibliographical references (p.) and index.
Contents: Before Europeans—Exploration and settlement—Becoming a colony—During the war—After the war and nationhood—Time line—Glossary terms.
  ISBN 1-56766-612-4 (alk. paper)
 1. Georgia—History—Colonial period, ca. 1600–1775—Juvenile literature. 2. Georgia—History—1775–1865—Juvenile literature. [1. Georgia—History—Colonial period, ca. 1600–1775. 2. Georgia—History—1775–1865.] I. Title. II. Series.
  F289.D25 2003
  975.8'02—dc21   2003003768

11/2003
Childsworld
28.50

Contents

Chapter ONE

The First Georgians

The dramatic mark left on the landscape by Georgia's Mound Builders is still visible today. The chief priests lived in temples at the top of the largest of these earthen mounds, which extend more than 3 acres (1.215 hectares) and rise to heights greater than 60 feet (18.3 meters).

PEOPLE LIVED IN NORTH AMERICA FOR THOUsands of years before the first Europeans arrived. Wandering hunters and farmers roamed the area as long ago as 9000 B.C. They made pottery and other objects.

Later, around A.D. 1000, a group we know as the Mound Builders lived in the area that would become Georgia. They are called Mound Builders because they built mounds of dirt and shells. Religious ceremonies took place around the mounds, and the dead were sometimes buried beneath them.

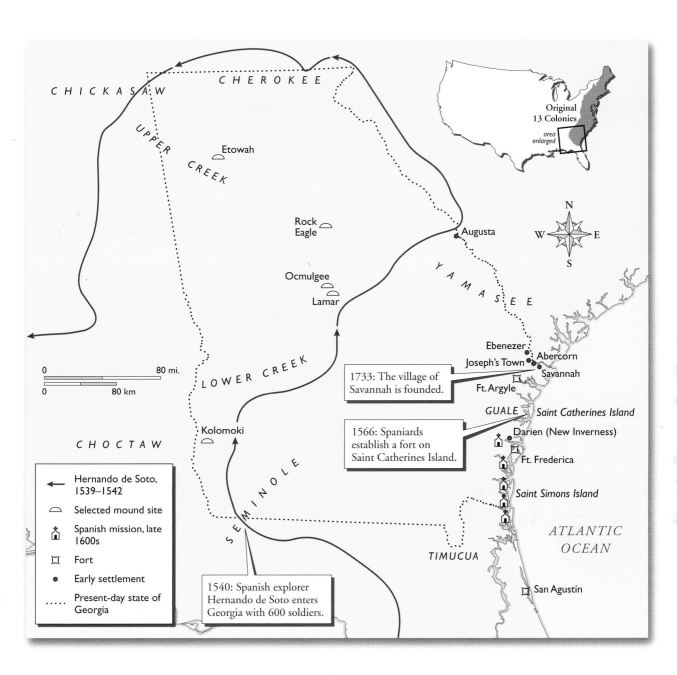

Georgia Colony at the time of the first European settlement

The Mound Builders were the **ancestors** of the Native Americans who lived in Georgia when the Europeans first arrived there. At that time, many different Native American groups lived in the area. The four main groups were

Tchaktas matachez en Guerriers qui portent des chevelures.

The Choctaw were known for their beautiful pottery, glass beadwork, leatherwork, and baskets woven from wood and swamp cane. Most of these traditional skills were handed down through the centuries and are still in use by modern-day Choctaws.

the Creek, the Cherokee, the Choctaw, and the Chickasaw.

The Creek had the most people. They lived in villages, and they farmed and hunted for their food.

Their crops included corn, beans, and squash. They hunted deer, rabbits, squirrels, and other animals. Their way of life included music, art, storytelling, religion, sports, and games.

The Cherokee were like the Creek in some ways. They were also farmers and hunters. But they often argued with the Creek over land. Sometimes the Creek and Cherokee fought, and sometimes they used peaceful means to settle their differences.

The Native Americans of Georgia first met Europeans in the 1500s. Those encounters would soon bring big changes to the land, the people who lived there, and the people who came to explore it.

8

IN THE 1700S, THE CREEK PEOPLE LIVED IN BETWEEN 50 AND 80 VILLAGES IN what are now the states of Georgia and Alabama. The larger Creek villages included a long, wide space called a plaza where ceremonies took place. The Creeks held meetings and received important guests there. Along the sides of the plaza were buildings like grandstands in a ballpark, with seats and a view of the plaza. In the summer months, Creek leaders watched the activity in the plaza from these buildings. The same activities were held indoors through the winter months.

Creek families tended to live together in the villages, building their homes close to one another. These family neighborhoods were called compounds. Usually, the compounds ran along a river or creek, which is why the British gave the Creek their name. The compounds also included gardens and fields for growing crops. Creek families were very close and shared the work and food.

Chapter Two

The Europeans Arrive

Christopher Columbus was the first European to "discover" the Americas. His claim of the land for Spain made the Spanish empire the largest in the world during the 16th century.

ITALIAN EXPLORER CHRISTOPHER COLUMBUS first set foot in the Americas in 1492 on an island in the Caribbean Sea he called San Salvador. Columbus's voyage had been paid for by Spain, which was looking for a faster

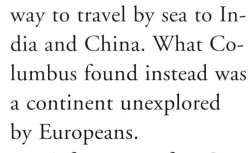

way to travel by sea to India and China. What Columbus found instead was a continent unexplored by Europeans.

A few years after Columbus's voyage, Spain sent explorers to North America to look for gold. In the next few decades, Spanish explorers and settlers spread into Cuba,

Mexico, South America, and Florida.

It was the search for gold that brought Spanish explorer Hernando de Soto into the Georgia area. In the spring of 1539, de Soto sailed from Cuba to Florida. He and 600 soldiers traveled north and entered Georgia in 1540.

As the Spaniards marched across the region, they cap-tured Native Americans and made them work as slaves. In the Georgia area, de Soto and his men met the Creek, who were friendly toward them and brought them food. But the Spaniards still forced many Creek into slavery.

Many more Creek died of diseases such as measles and smallpox, which the Europeans brought to the Americas. Native Americans had never before come in contact with these diseases, so their bodies could not fight them. Many thousands of Native Americans died in what would become Georgia, and millions died in all of North America.

Hernando de Soto was lured into the interior of America by the tales he had heard of vast riches to be found there. He had already made a fortune in gold as one of the conquerors of the Incan Empire in Peru, but he never found the gold he was looking for in America.

Interesting Fact

▸ Some Creek and Cher-okee Indians fought with the British against the Americans in the Revolutionary War.

De Soto's expedition up the Mississippi brought deadly European diseases to the natives of many different tribes along the way. Many natives were enslaved by the Spaniards, as well.

De Soto and his troops never found gold in Georgia or anywhere else they explored. In the spring of 1542, de Soto died in what is today the state of Louisiana and was buried in the Mississippi River.

The Spaniards established a fort in Georgia on Saint Catherine's Island in 1566. Soon afterward, the Spanish built more villages and forts along the Georgia coast. Georgia was important to Spain because it was located next to the land it claimed called Florida.

Now in control of Florida and Georgia, the Spanish brought in priests to teach the Native Americans about Christianity. During the late 1500s, the Spanish built small settlements and churches along the Georgia coast. At this time, the Spanish called the land Guale, named after a local

Interesting Fact

▸ Slavery and rum, an alcoholic drink, were banned from the Georgia colony when it was founded.

Saint Catherine's Island was the first important Spanish fort in the area that would later become Georgia.

13

▶ Just after the Spaniards raised their first cross on Saint Catherine's Island, a huge rainstorm broke out, ending a drought. This helped them spread their religion among the Gaule people.

Saint Ignatius of Loyola founded the Society of Jesus, or Jesuits, who made it their mission to convert the natives ruled by the Spanish Empire in the Americas.

Native American group. Very few Spaniards settled in this area, however.

In the early 1600s, the British started traveling to North America from across the Atlantic Ocean. The first permanent English settlement in North America was established in Jamestown, Virginia, in 1607.

At this time, many people in England were not allowed to practice their religion.

To find a place where they could have religious freedom, a group founded a colony in Massachusetts in 1620. Other English people came to America to get more land, to build farms, and to start new lives.

The English also went to Georgia in large numbers. With lots of empty land, Georgia was a good place to start a farm. As more people from England and other

The English settlement of Jamestown (below) posed a threat to the Spanish, who had already been in the Americas for at least 40 years and had settlements in Georgia and the southern regions of North America.

▶ In the 1600s, there were few decent tools for farming. Many farmers had only axes to clear the land and hoes or other crude and simple tools to dig the earth. Most did not even own plows.

European nations moved there, Spain lost control of Georgia. In 1629, Britain claimed Georgia as its own.

In the early 1600s, English colonists poured into the wilds of Georgia, driving out the Spanish and allowing King Charles I to claim the territory in the name of England.

SPAIN, FRANCE, AND ENGLAND ALL EXPLORED THE EAST COAST OF NORTH America in the late 1500s and 1600s. All three countries were looking for more land. The Europeans wanted to become rich by sending goods and crops back to Europe.

But each nation had different goals in Georgia. The Spaniards were looking for gold. They established a few forts and churches in Georgia. The British, helped by the Creek and the Cherokee, drove out most of the Spaniards by the 1700s. The few French settlers in Georgia had left France because they had been harassed for being Protestant in a Catholic country. They did not build towns or farms in Georgia. Nor did they look for gold as the Spaniards did.

The British who came to Georgia wanted to create a more permanent life for themselves. They cleared land for farms and built homes. They gathered together to live in small villages that would later grow into larger towns. By the time Georgia became a colony in 1732, many British farmers and settlers were already living there.

Chapter THREE

Becoming a Colony

Debtor's prison wasn't as harsh as prison for criminals. But the people sent there were rarely released before their debts were paid in full—and few were able to pay those debts.

THE BRITISH COLONY OF GEORGIA MIGHT not have been founded if life in 18th-century Britain had been better. In Britain in those days, if you owed money and couldn't pay, you were put in prison. These were called debtors' prisons. Once a person went in, he seldom got out.

An Englishman named James Edward Oglethorpe fought against the debtors' prisons. He wanted to send the prisoners to America for a new start. Oglethorpe was a member of **Parliament.** He was a

respected man and had many important friends. He was therefore able to convince Britain's King George II to give him and his friends a large piece of land in America. They named the land Georgia, after the king who gave it to them.

In the spring of 1732, King George II signed a paper called a **charter,** founding Georgia. Twenty-one men, called trustees, would govern the new colony, which lay between the colonies of Florida and South Carolina. The British hoped that Georgia would protect these settlements from the French in Louisiana to the west and the Spanish in Florida to the south.

Reports of the new colony appeared in British newspapers. Anyone who wanted to come to Georgia was told to apply to the **trustees.** Many people

James Oglethorpe joined the British army at the age of 14 and became a member of the British Parliament at the age of 26.

Oglethorpe first arrived in what is now Georgia with not quite 120 settlers, including a doctor and a preacher. These early colonists had hopes of outlawing liquor and slavery, and their relationship with the Native Americans living there was friendly.

Interesting Fact

▶ It was Oglethorpe's idea to build each block of homes around a common green. This unique and beautiful feature is still a part of Savannah today.

applied, but only about 120 from 35 families were allowed into the first settlement. More would come later.

Poor people and those who wanted religious freedom were among the first people to move to Georgia. The trustees paid for the journey of some people who couldn't pay their own way. The trustees also gave them food and supplies and 50 acres (20.25 ha) of land for farming. People who had the money to pay their own way to Georgia were given 500 acres (202.5 ha) of land.

In 1733, Oglethorpe arrived in Georgia and established the village of Savannah along the Atlantic Ocean. The name came either from the Sawana Indians or from the Spanish word *sábana,* which means "flat country." Savannah was divided into squares, which served as parks, pens for livestock, and other purposes. The streets were straight, and each family had a house with a garden. Savannah became the capital of Georgia and its largest settlement. Oglethorpe also established other cities and a series of forts to defend the colony against the French and the Spanish.

Many of Georgia's early colonists were farmers. They grew crops such as corn, rice, and vegetables. Settlers also hoped that Georgia's wild mulberry trees would produce silkworms for the making of silk. But the silk business never became important, and soon landowners started growing cotton.

Georgia was the youngest of the 13 American colonies, and it had the smallest population. In 1750, fewer than 5,000 European settlers lived there. Georgia was also the

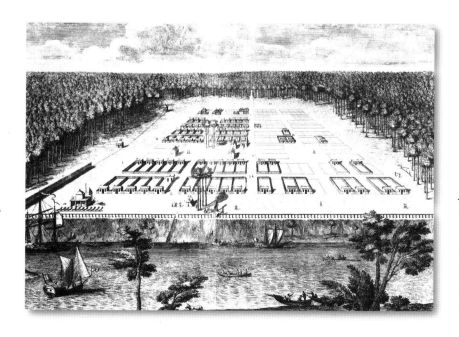

Oglethorpe laid the plan for the city of Savannah with the help of Colonel William Bull. It was one of the first planned cities in North America and much of its original design remains the same today.

As the demand for cotton fabric increased in England, growing cotton quickly became the most important industry in Georgia.

poorest colony. Almost one-third of the population had a difficult time earning enough money for food and supplies. Besides farmers, the colony was home to fur traders, carpenters, merchants, doctors, and others. But even many of these people had farms to grow food for their own use.

Early on, Georgia had a small number of **plantations.** Cotton was the most common plantation crop. As cotton became more valuable, the number of plantations in Georgia grew.

As more of Georgia's land was used for plantations, the forests had to be cleared. The trees were used as building material. Early homes and churches in Georgia were often built of wood.

Most early settlers in Georgia had British roots. But people of many other backgrounds also lived there. People came from Austria, France, Germany, Ireland, Italy, Portugal, Scotland, Spain, and Switzerland.

WHEN JAMES OGLETHORPE FOUNDED GEORGIA, HE DID NOT PERMIT SLAVERY in the colony. But as cotton became a more important crop, the colonists began demanding that slavery be allowed. Many workers were needed to plant and harvest cotton and to remove seeds from the picked cotton. The Georgians said they could not compete with cotton growers in other colonies if they were not allowed to use slaves for this work. In 1750, slavery was made legal in Georgia.

Once cotton became a major crop and slavery became legal, the number of plantations increased. Soon there were thousands of African-American slaves in Georgia. Most of them lived and worked on plantations. Many white Georgians grew wealthy using slave labor. By the time of the American Revolution, about half of the 40,000 settlers in Georgia were enslaved African-Americans.

The American Revolution

IN THE 1700S, BRITAIN AND FRANCE ARGUED over the rich farmland and fur trade in the Ohio River valley. In 1754, this argument

Many Native Americans fought alongside the French. But others sided with the British.

24

turned into the French and Indian War. When the British finally won the war in 1763, they gained all land east of the Mississippi River as well as Canada. The war had been very expensive for Britain. The British started taxing the colonies to pay for the costs of the war.

The first tax was called the Stamp Act. It required that all printed material, including newspapers, legal documents, and even playing cards, carry a special stamp. The colonists had to buy these stamps. All across the colonies, people began protesting this tax. They sent letters to Britain complaining. The colonists believed that if they were going to be taxed, they should also have representation

After the French and Indian War, members of the British House of Commons, shown above, determined that the colonists should pay a series of taxes to help lessen the costs of the war.

The cotton business brought great wealth to the large landowners in Georgia and strengthened their ties to Britain. Social life on the large plantations included balls, parties, and formal dinners in rooms such as this one.

in Parliament. But the colonists had no place in Britain's government.

In 1765, nine of the 13 colonies sent representatives to New York City to plan a way of dealing with the tax problem. Georgia did not send representatives to the meeting. In general, Georgians did not complain as much about the taxes as people in other colonies. Trade with Britain had made many Georgia landowners rich. Because of this, they did not want to fight the British.

In 1766, Britain ended the Stamp Act but soon passed even more taxes. The colonists became angrier with each new tax. Among the items taxed were tea and sugar. In 1773, a group of Massachusetts colonists snuck aboard some ships in Boston Harbor and dumped boxes of tea into the water. This protest of the tea tax is known as the Boston Tea Party. Many more protests followed.

People in the colonies were dividing into two groups. One group was loyal to Britain. They were called the Loyalists. Georgia had the largest group of Loyalists of all the colonies. The settlers' children, who were born in the colony, were more likely to favor independence from Britain. People who supported American independence were called Patriots.

In time, anger over the taxes turned into a war against Britain. The fighting started

Word of the Boston Tea Party encouraged other Patriots to defy British control. But Loyalists such as those in Georgia were outraged by these rebellious acts.

on April 19, 1775, with small battles at the towns of Lexington and Concord in Massachusetts. The following year, British warships attacked Savannah. The Revolutionary War was on. On July 4, 1776, representatives from the colonies approved the Declaration of Independence.

The attack on Savannah was hard on the British, but it was much harder on the colonists. Britain's control of Savannah didn't end until close to the end of the Revolutionary War itself.

The war, however, was far from over. British troops moved through Georgia, capturing many towns. In 1778, British ships captured Savannah. French troops joined the American troops and tried to recapture the city in 1779. But Savannah was not freed until a battle in 1782. In 1783, the war finally ended. The colonies were at last independent.

IN THE 1700S IN GEORGIA, WOMEN'S LIVES CENTERED ON THE HOME. THEY cooked, made clothes, tended to the family's animals and garden, and raised children. Abigail Minis did all of that and much more.

In 1733, Abigail and her husband, Abraham, were on the first boat filled with Jewish settlers to arrive in Georgia. They had moved from London, England, to Georgia because they were looking for somewhere to practice their religion in peace. They settled in Savannah, where Abraham set up a trading business.

In time, Abigail gave birth to nine children. Then, when Abraham died in 1757, she took over the family business. In the coming years, she expanded the family's land holdings from 500 acres (203 ha) to 2,500 acres (1013 ha). Her trading business expanded as well, and she opened a tavern.

Unlike many wealthy Georgians, Abigail Minis was a Patriot. During the Revolution, she provided American troops with food and supplies. She lived until 1794, long enough to see a new nation born.

Becoming a Nation

NOW THAT THEY WERE INDEPENDENT, THE colonies had to come together as a new nation. During the Revolution, the 13 colonies had united under an agreement called the **Articles of Confederation.**

Under this document, the states acted almost as if they were separate countries. The central government had very little power. It needed money for the work of government but was not allowed to impose taxes. When the central government asked the states for money, most did not help. The new nation could not pay what it owed. Nor was there any court system to decide legal matters. Each state made its own agreements with foreign countries. And the new states argued with one another over many matters, including their borders.

To solve these problems, representatives from the states met in Philadelphia, Pennsylvania, in May 1787. They decided to scrap the Articles of Confederation and write a new **constitution.** The representatives from Georgia included Abraham Baldwin, William Houstoun, and William Few. After much discussion, the U.S. Constitution was written.

The new Constitution provided for a much stronger central government. The new government had its own courts and could pass taxes. Only the central government would make agreements with other countries.

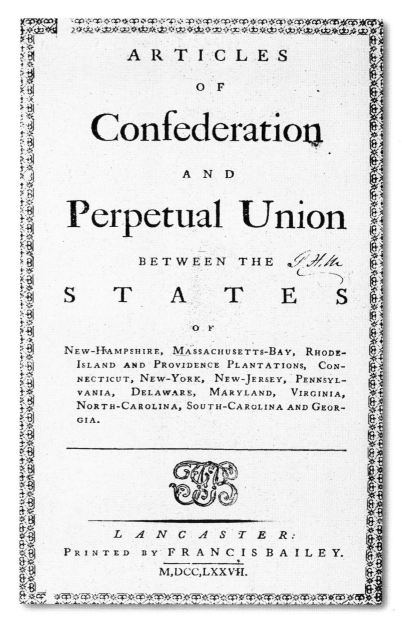

ARTICLES

OF

Confederation

AND

Perpetual Union

BETWEEN THE

STATES

OF

NEW-HAMPSHIRE, MASSACHUSETTS-BAY, RHODE-ISLAND AND PROVIDENCE PLANTATIONS, CONNECTICUT, NEW-YORK, NEW-JERSEY, PENNSYLVANIA, DELAWARE, MARYLAND, VIRGINIA, NORTH-CAROLINA, SOUTH-CAROLINA AND GEORGIA.

LANCASTER:
PRINTED BY FRANCIS BAILEY.
M,DCC,LXXVII.

The Articles of Confederation represented America's first organized attempt at self-government as a group of united states.

Some people worried that the Constitution gave the government too much power. Their concerns were answered when a list of personal rights was added to the Constitution. This list, called the Bill of Rights, grants Americans many rights, including freedom of religion and freedom of speech.

On January 1, 1788, Georgia became the fourth state to approve the Constitution.

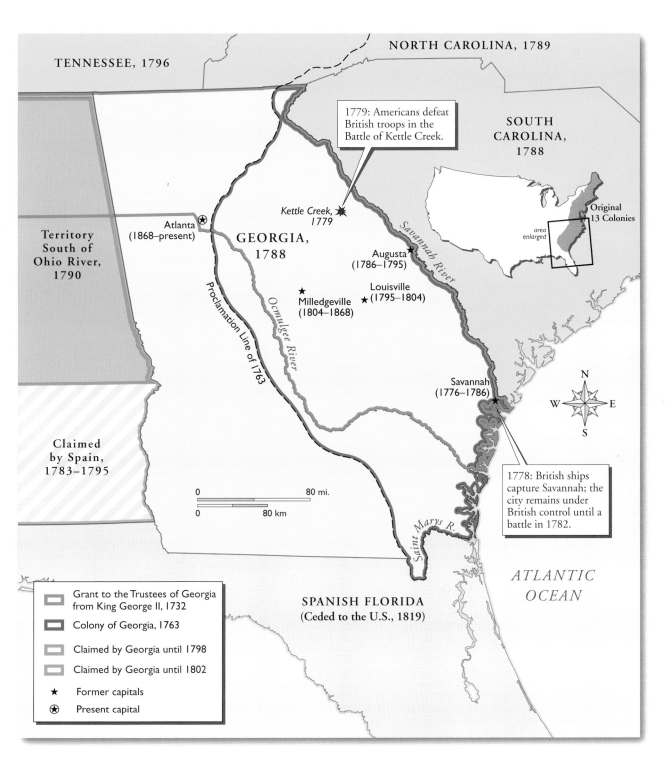

TENNESSEE, 1796

NORTH CAROLINA, 1789

SOUTH CAROLINA, 1788

1779: Americans defeat British troops in the Battle of Kettle Creek.

Original 13 Colonies

area enlarged

Territory South of Ohio River, 1790

Atlanta (1868–present)

GEORGIA, 1788

Kettle Creek, 1779

Augusta (1786–1795)

Savannah River

Louisville (1795–1804)

Proclamation Line of 1763

Milledgeville (1804–1868)

Ocmulgee River

Claimed by Spain, 1783–1795

0   80 mi.
0   80 km

Savannah (1776–1786)

N
W   E
S

1778: British ships capture Savannah; the city remains under British control until a battle in 1782.

Saint Marys R.

ATLANTIC OCEAN

SPANISH FLORIDA (Ceded to the U.S., 1819)

Grant to the Trustees of Georgia from King George II, 1732

Colony of Georgia, 1763

Claimed by Georgia until 1798

Claimed by Georgia until 1802

★ Former capitals

⊛ Present capital

Georgia Colony before statehood

33

Americans had formed a strong government with laws they agreed upon. The states were now united as a single nation.

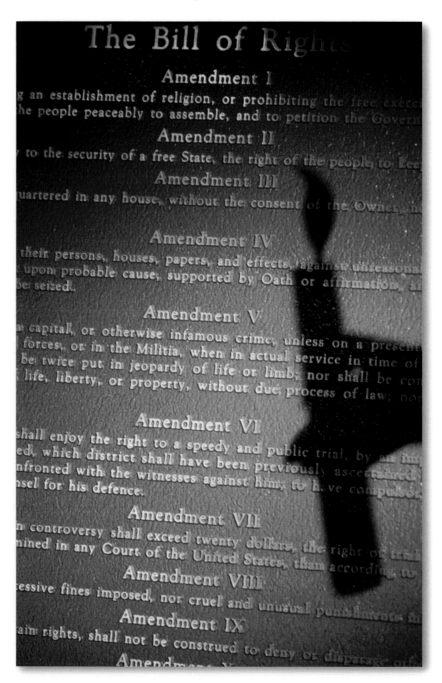

America's Bill of Rights is still an important part of democratic freedoms in the United States today.

AT THE TIME GEORGIA BECAME THE FOURTH STATE IN THE UNION, IN 1788, Augusta was the capital city. But it was the second city in the state to have that distinction. The first, beginning in 1777, was Oglethorpe's beautiful Savannah. The capital was switched back and forth between Savannah and Augusta several times over the next 10 years, until on February 22, 1785, Savannah saw its last meeting of Georgia's General Assembly. From that point on Augusta remained the official capital until 1796.

Augusta had also been founded by Oglethorpe, in 1735, and by 1788, it was home to a rapidly growing population. There were no trains at the time and other types of transportation were slow and unreliable, so having a conveniently-located capital was important. This was because, unlike today, in those years many simple legal procedures had to go through the state legislature, including name changes, divorces, and the approval of land grants.

In 1868, Atlanta became Georgia's capital, which it has remained ever since. The building's golden dome is topped by a copper statue of a woman usually referred to as Miss Freedom or the Goddess of Liberty. In her hands she holds a sword and a torch. At night her torch is lit, reminding Georgians of the part their state played in the country's early struggle for freedom.

1400s Creek, Cherokee, Choctaw, Chickasaw, and many other Native Americans live in the region that will become Georgia.

1540 Spanish explorer Hernando de Soto enters Georgia.

1566 Spaniards establish a fort in Georgia on Saint Catherine's Island.

1629 The British claim ownership of Georgia.

1732 The colony of Georgia is founded.

1733 Savannah becomes the first British settlement in Georgia.

1763 Britain defeats France in the French and Indian War.

1765 The British pass the Stamp Act, a tax on the colonists.

1766 The Stamp Act is ended.

1774 The First Continental Congress is held in Philadelphia. Georgia is the only colony not to send representatives to the meeting.

1775 The American Revolution begins.

1776 On July 4, the Declaration of Independence is adopted.

1778 British ships capture Savannah.

1782 Savannah is freed from the British.

1783 The American Revolution ends.

1788 Georgia becomes the fourth state to approve the U.S. Constitution.

1789 George Washington becomes the first president of the United States.

Glossary TERMS

ancestors (AN-sess-tuhrs)
Ancestors are relatives from a long time ago. The Mound Builders were the ancestors of the Creek and Cherokee.

Articles of Confederation (AR-tuh-kuhls uv kon-fed-uh-RAY-shun)
The Articles of Confederation was the first constitution for the United States. It was replaced by the U.S. Constitution in 1788.

charter (CHAR-tuhr)
A charter is a document giving settlers permission to form a colony. King George II signed the charter founding Georgia in 1732.

constitution (kon-stuh-TOO-shun)
A constitution is a document outlining the structure and basic laws of a government. Georgia was the fourth state to approve the U.S. Constitution.

Parliament (PAR-luh-muhnt)
Parliament is the lawmaking body of Great Britain. After the French and Indian War, Parliament began passing taxes on the American colonies.

plantations (plan-TAY-shuns)
Plantations were large farms that grew a single important crop and usually used enslaved workers. Most Georgia plantations grew cotton.

trustees (truss-TEES)
Trustees are people in charge of running something. Twenty-two trustees governed the Georgia colony.

Georgia Colony's FOUNDING FATHERS

Abraham Baldwin (1754–1807)
Congress of Confederation delegate, 1785; Continental Congress delegate, 1785, 1787–89; Constitutional Convention delegate, 1787; U.S. Constitution signer; U.S. House of Representative member, 1790–99; U.S. senator, 1799–1807

William Few (1748–1828)
Continental Congress delegate, 1780–85; Constitutional Convention delegate, 1787; U.S. Constitution signer; U.S. senator, 1789–93; state court justice, 1796–99; New York state assembly member, 1802–1805

Button Gwinnett (1735?–1777)
Continental Congress delegate, 1776, 1777; Declaration of Independence signer, 1776; Georgia president, 1777

Lyman Hall (1724–1790)
Continental Congress delegate, 1775–78, 1780; Declaration of Independence signer; Georgia president, 1783

William Houstoun (1755–1813)
Continental Congress delegate, 1783–86; Constitutional Convention delegate, 1787

Edward Langworthy (1738–1802)
Continental Congress delegate, 1777; Articles of Confederation signer, 1777

William L. Pierce (1740–1789)
Continental Congress delegate, 1786; Constitutional Convention delegate, 1787

Edward Telfair (1735–1807)
Articles of Confederation signer, 1777; Continental Congress delegate, 1778, 1780–82; Georgia governor, 1789–93

George Walton (1741?–1804)
Continental Congress delegate, 1776–79, 1781; Declaration of Independence signer; Articles of Confederation signer; Georgia governor, 1779–80, 1789; Georgia chief justice, 1783–89; Georgia superior court justice, 1790–92, 1793–95, 1799–1804; U.S. senator, 1795–96

John Walton (1738–1783)
Articles of Confederation signer, 1777; Continental Congress delegate, 1778

For Further INFORMATION

Web Sites

Visit our homepage for lots of links about the Georgia colony:
http://www.childsworld.com/links.html

Note to Parents, Teachers, and Librarians:
We routinely verify our Web links to make sure they're safe,
active sites—so encourage your readers to check them out!

Books

Collier, Christopher, and James Lincoln Collier. *Clash of Cultures: Prehistory–1638.* New York: Benchmark Books, 1998.

Fradin, Dennis Brindell. *The Georgia Colony.* Chicago: Children's Press, 1990.

Girod, Christina M. *Native Americans of the Southeast.* San Diego: Lucent Books, 2001.

Masters, Nancy Robinson. *Georgia.* New York: Children's Press, 1999.

Otfinoski, Steve. *Georgia.* New York: Benchmark Books, 2001.

Scordato, Ellen. *The Creek Indians.* New York: Chelsea House, 1993.

Places to Visit or Contact

The Augusta Museum of History
To learn about the history of the region from the time people first arrived there 12,000 years ago
560 Reynolds Street
Augusta, GA 30901
706/722-8485

The Georgia Historical Society
For all kinds of information about Georgia's history
501 Whitaker Street
Savannah, GA 31401
912/651-2125

Index

About the Author

MARC DAVIS IS A FORMER NEWSPAPER REPORTER, THE AUTHOR of two novels, and a freelance journalist specializing in business, medical, historical, and cultural subjects. His writing-reporting has appeared in national publications and on the Internet. He attended the University of Illinois, Chicago, and New York University. Davis lives in a Chicago suburb.